THE MINDFULNESS
JOURNEYS
COLORING BOOK

THE MINDFULNESS
JOURNEYS
COLORING BOOK

Get Lost in an Adult Coloring Adventure

MARIO MARTÍN

THE EXPERIMENT

NEW YORK

THE MINDFULNESS JOURNEYS COLORING BOOK:
Get Lost in an Adult Coloring Adventure
Copyright © 2024 by Mario Martín

The Experiment, LLC
220 East 23rd Street, Suite 600
New York, NY 10010-4658
theexperimentpublishing.com

THE EXPERIMENT and its colophon
are registered trademarks of
The Experiment, LLC.

The Experiment's books are available at special
discounts when purchased in bulk for
premiums and sales promotions as well as for
fundraising or educational use. For details, contact us at
info@theexperimentpublishing.com.

Library of Congress Cataloging-in-Publication Data
available upon request

ISBN 978-1-891011-64-1

Cover design by Beth Bugler
Author photograph courtesy of the author

Manufactured in the United States of America

First printing November 2024
10 9 8 7 6 5 4 3 2 1

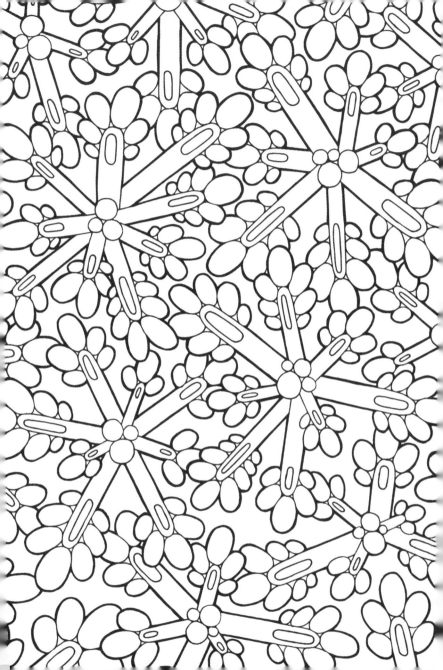

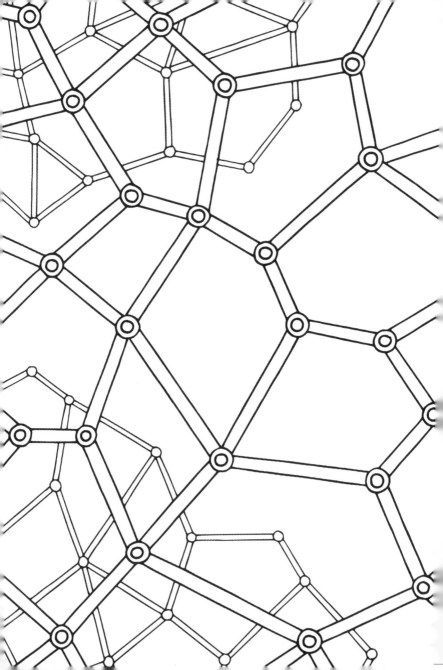

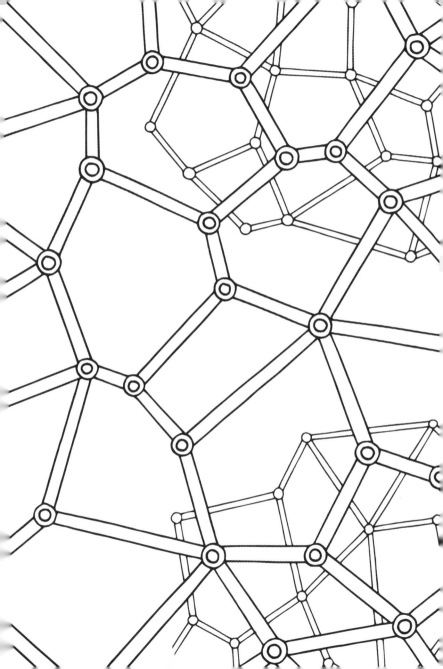

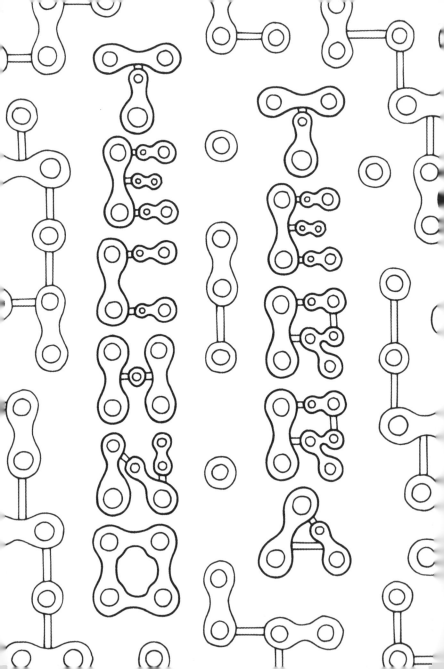

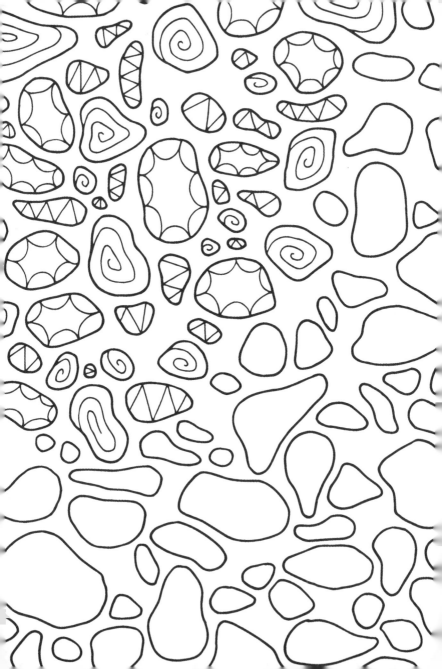

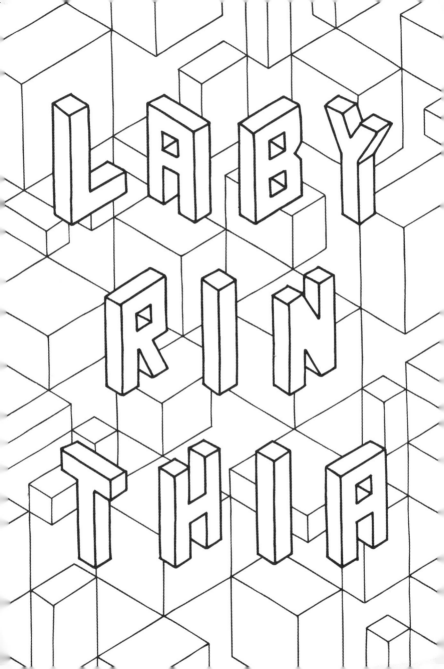

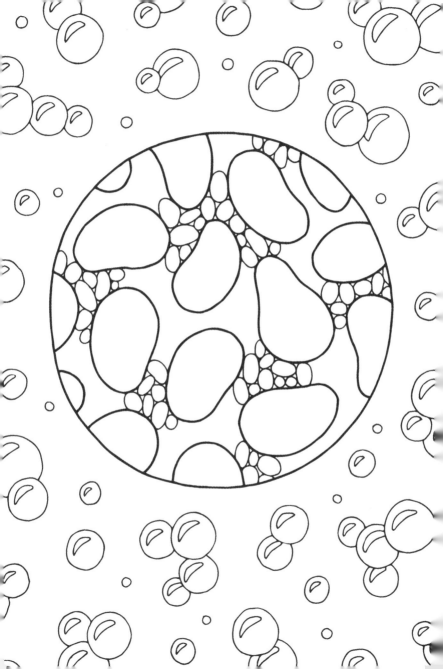

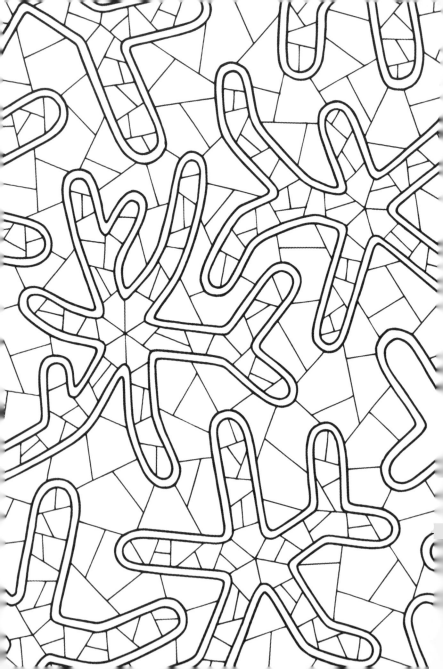

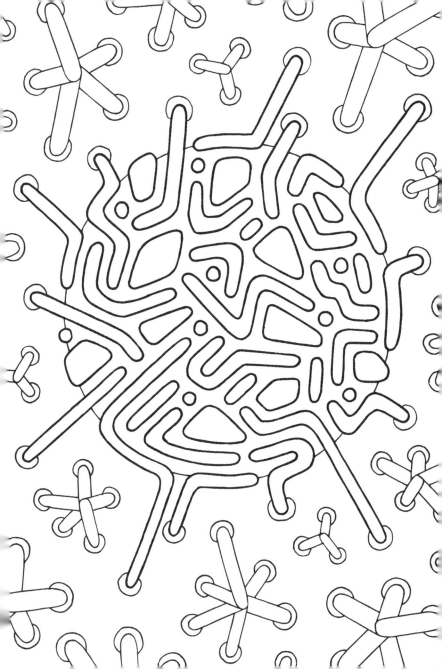

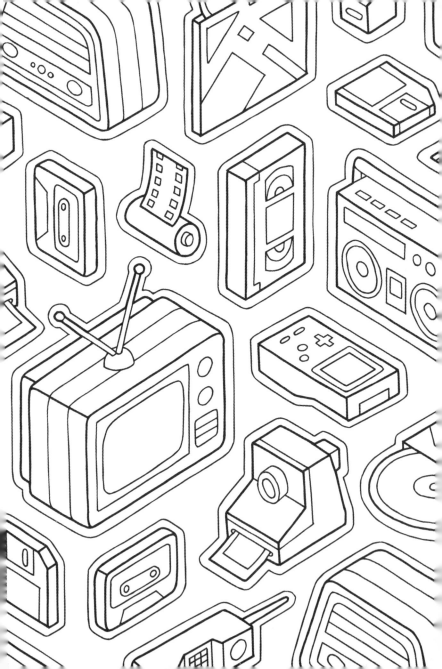

~ Your turn to doodle ~

∽ Continue coloring with ∽

Trade Paperback Originals • $9.95 US | $12.95 CAN • 112 pages

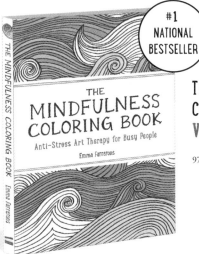

THE MINDFULNESS COLORING BOOK
VOLUME ONE

978-1-61519-282-3

THE MINDFULNESS COLORING BOOK
VOLUME TWO

978-1-61519-302-8

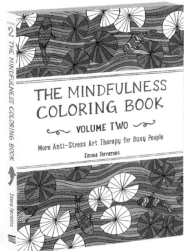